OCT – 2012

PIRATES! PIRATES! PIRATES!

Life Under the Pirate Code

BY CINDY JENSON-ELLIOTT

Reading Consultant:
Barbara J. Fox
Reading Specialist
Professor Emerita
North Carolina State University

CAPSTONE PRESS
a capstone imprint

Blazers is published by Capstone Press,
1710 Roe Crest Drive, North Mankato, Minnesota 56003.
www.capstonepub.com

Library of Congress Cataloging-in-Publication Data
Jenson-Elliott, Cynthia L.
    Life under the pirate code / by Cindy Jenson-Elliott.
        p. cm.—(Blazers)
    Includes bibliographical references and index.
    Summary: "Describes how a code of rules guided life onboard a pirate ship and
punishments for breaking the rules"—Provided by publisher.
    ISBN 978-1-4296-8611-2 (library binding)
    ISBN 978-1-62065-201-5 (ebook PDF)
    1. Pirates—Juvenile literature. I. Title.
G535.J44 2013
910.4'5—dc23   2011048907

Editorial Credits

Aaron Sautter, editor; Veronica Correia, designer; Marcie Spence, media researcher;
    Laura Manthe, production specialist

Photo Credits

Bridgeman Art Library: asapworldwide.com, 25, Bibliotheque des Arts Decoratifs, Paris, France/
Archives Charmet, 19, Ferris, Jean Leon Gerome, 5, Howard Pyle Collection/Deleware Art
Museum, Wilmington, 14, International, 17, Look and Learn, cover, 8, 10, Peter Newark
Historical Pictures, 7, 20; Image Works, The: Fotomas/TopFoto, 13; Mary Evans Picture Library,
27; Paul Daly, 23; Rick Reeves, Tampa, FL: 28–29; Shutterstock: Maugli, cover

Capstone Press would like to thank Alex Diaz at the St. Augustine Pirate and Treasure Museum
for his help in creating this book.

Printed in the United States of America in Stevens Point, Wisconsin.

032012   006678WZF12

Table of Contents

Honor among Thieves

Pirates led wild lives in the Golden Age of Piracy (1690–1730). They raided ships, **kidnapped** people, and stole treasure. Pirates on each ship lived by a set of rules called a code.

kidnap—to capture someone and hold him or her as a prisoner until demands are met

Chapter One

Roles and Rights

THE CAPTAIN

Ship codes stated each pirate's **role** on the ship. During battles the captain's orders were followed without question. At other times the captain worked with the crew to make decisions.

role—a person's job and duties

Fact

A pirate "council of equals" voted to pick a captain. Pirates could also vote to replace a captain.

Fact

The quartermaster usually got 1½ shares of any treasure taken. If a ship was taken as a prize, he could become its new captain.

THE QUARTERMASTER AND BOATSWAIN

The quartermaster was second in command. He was in charge of the crew and punished rule breakers. The **boatswain** kept the ship in good shape. He put the crew to work to fix the ship.

boatswain—a ship's officer who is responsible for maintaining the ship

Fact

Captured workers were given papers to show they were forced to join the crew. If they were caught and put on trial, these papers could help set them free.

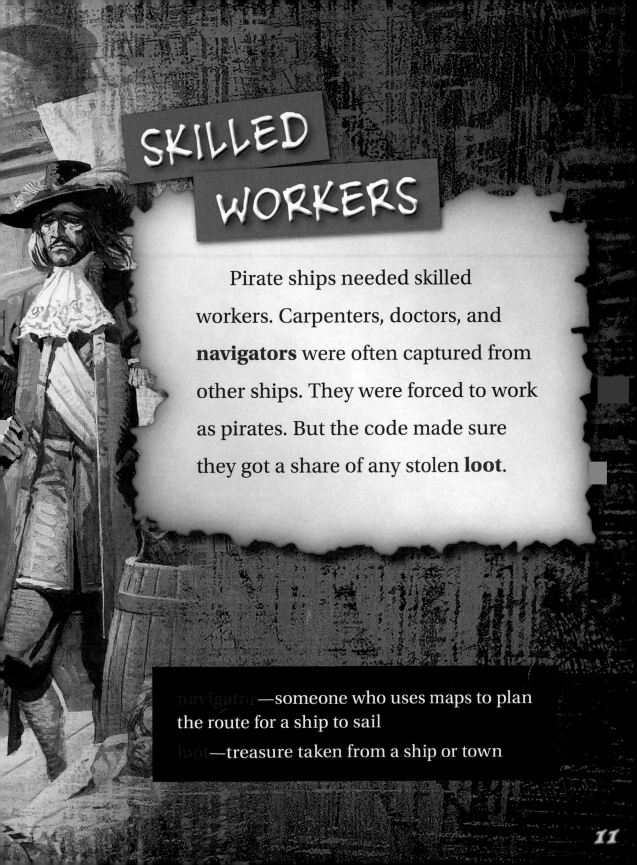

SKILLED WORKERS

Pirate ships needed skilled workers. Carpenters, doctors, and **navigators** were often captured from other ships. They were forced to work as pirates. But the code made sure they got a share of any stolen **loot**.

navigator—someone who uses maps to plan the route for a ship to sail

loot—treasure taken from a ship or town

Chapter Two

Rules for Daily Life

Some rules related to everyday life on a ship. Fires were always a danger on wooden ships. Pirates were not allowed to carry lighted candles below deck.

Fact

Pirates were not supposed to gamble on the ship. But many pirates gambled anyway.

Fact

The pirate code gave crew members rights they did not have on navy or merchant ships. A pirate could one day become a captain. Poor navy sailors had little chance of becoming a captain.

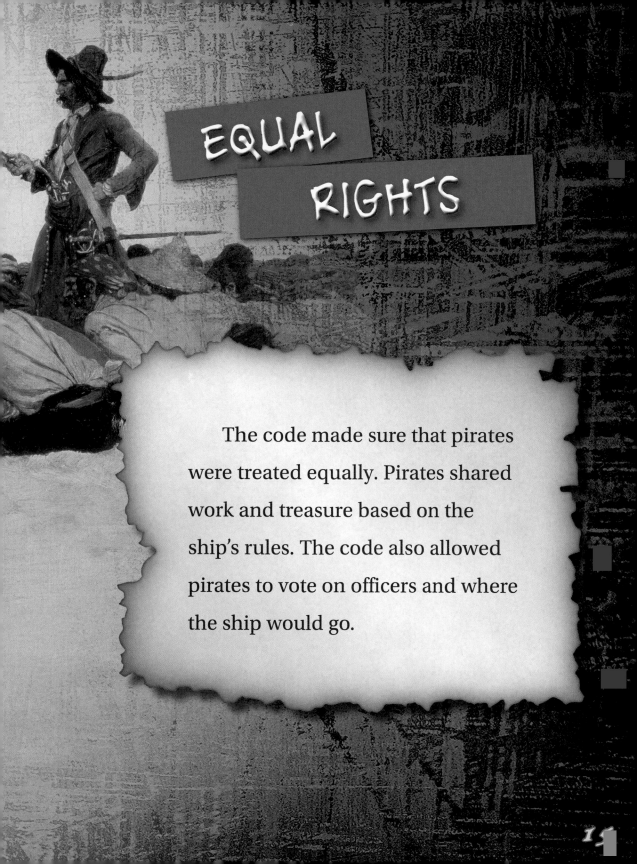

EQUAL RIGHTS

The code made sure that pirates were treated equally. Pirates shared work and treasure based on the ship's rules. The code also allowed pirates to vote on officers and where the ship would go.

Chapter Three

Rules in Battle

The pirate code kept pirates ready for battle. Pirates had to keep their weapons clean and ready to use at all times. Some ship rules said that no pirate could leave his post during a battle.

On one ship, no one was allowed
to leave until the crew had earned
a total of 1,000 British pounds.
Today that equals about $280,000.

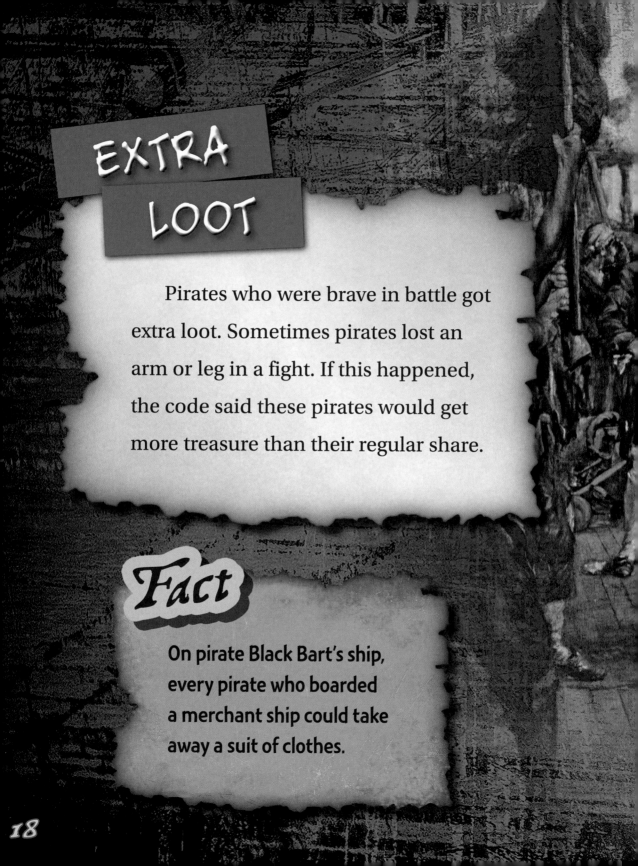

EXTRA LOOT

Pirates who were brave in battle got extra loot. Sometimes pirates lost an arm or leg in a fight. If this happened, the code said these pirates would get more treasure than their regular share.

Fact

On pirate Black Bart's ship, every pirate who boarded a merchant ship could take away a suit of clothes.

19

AFTER THE BATTLE

The rules listed special rewards for some pirates. Sometimes the first pirate to see a merchant ship was given the best pistol from that ship.

Fact

Pirate treasure often included Spanish silver coins called pieces of eight. Gold coins were called doubloons.

Chapter Four

Breaking the Rules

The ship's code was not kind to rule breakers. Pirates who didn't follow orders faced harsh punishments. They could be **flogged**, **keelhauled**, or killed.

flog—to beat with a whip

keelhaul—to attach a rope to someone and drag him or her under a ship as a punishment

Fact

Pirate crews often voted on which punishment a rule breaker should get.

DISAGREEMENTS

Pirates were not allowed to fight each other on the ship. If pirates had an argument, they went to shore to **duel**. The first pirate to wound the other usually won.

duel—a fight between two people using swords or guns

Fighting was not allowed because it disrupted the peace and kept the crew from their daily duties.

STEALING FROM OTHER PIRATES

Loyalty and trust were important to pirates. The code said that no pirate could steal loot from his shipmates. Pirates who broke this rule could be **marooned**.

maroon—to punish someone by leaving him or her alone on a deserted island

Fact

A marooned pirate was usually given only a pistol, gunpowder, one bullet, and a knife.

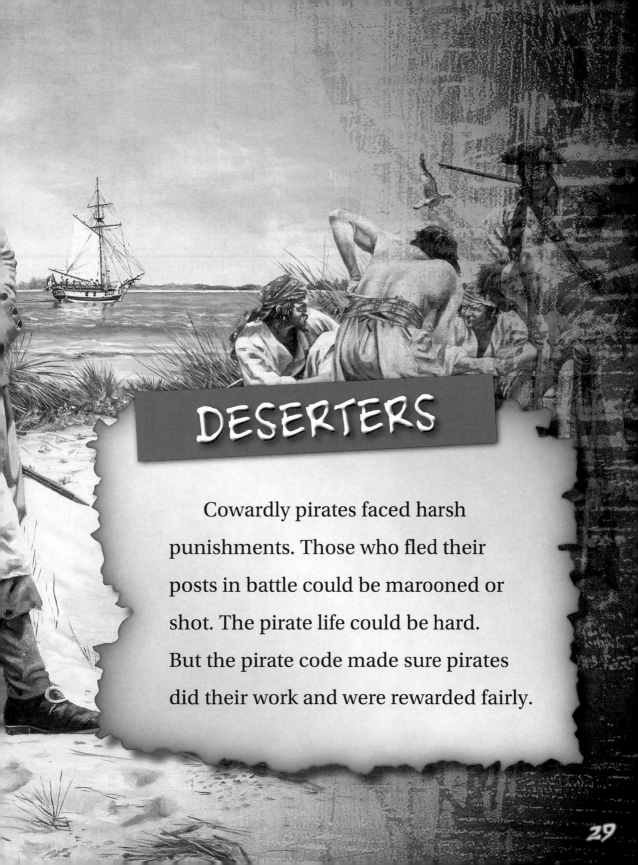

DESERTERS

Cowardly pirates faced harsh punishments. Those who fled their posts in battle could be marooned or shot. The pirate life could be hard. But the pirate code made sure pirates did their work and were rewarded fairly.

Glossary

boatswain (BOHT-sweyn)—a ship's officer who is responsible for maintaining the ship

council (KOUN-suhl)—a governing group of people who make decisions for a larger group

duel (DOO-uhl)—a fight between two people using swords or guns, fought according to strict rules

flog (FLOG)—to beat with a whip

keelhaul (KEEL-hawl)—to attach a rope to someone and drag him or her under the bottom of a ship

kidnap (KID-nap)—to capture someone and hold him or her as a prisoner until demands are met

loot (LOOT)—treasure taken from a ship or town

maroon (muh-ROON)—to punish someone by leaving him or her alone on a deserted island

navigator (NAV-uh-gay-tuhr)—someone who uses maps to plan the route for a ship to sail

pound (POUND)—a unit of money used in England

role (ROHL)—a person's job and duties

Read More

Biskup, Agnieszka. *Captured by Pirates!: An Isabel Soto History Adventure.* Graphic Expeditions. Mankato, Minn.: Capstone Press, 2012.

Claybourne, Anna. *Pirate Secrets Revealed.* Extreme Explorations! Mankato, Minn.: Capstone Press, 2010.

Platt, Richard. *Pirate.* Eyewitness Books. New York: DK Pub., 2007.

Internet Sites

FactHound offers a safe, fun way to find Internet sites related to this book. All of the sites on FactHound have been researched by our staff.

Here's all you do:

Visit *www.facthound.com*

Type in this code: 9781429686112

Super-cool stuff! Check out projects, games and lots more at **www.capstonekids.com**

Index